Time to SING

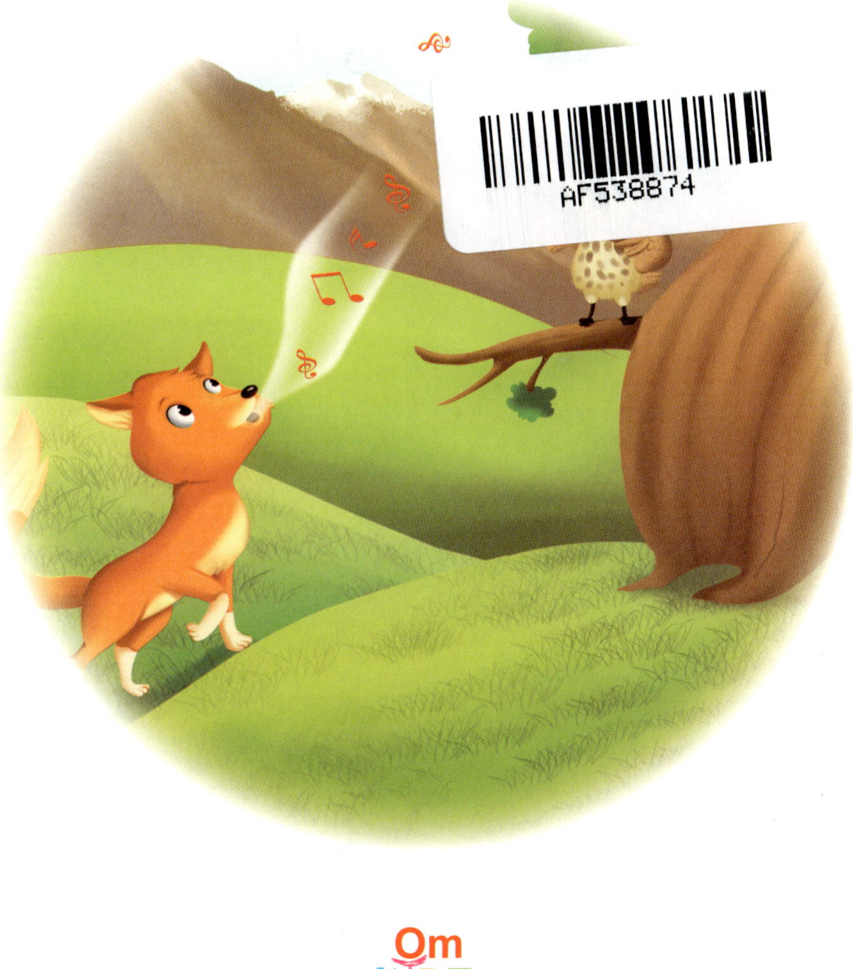

Om
KIDZ
An imprint of Om Books International

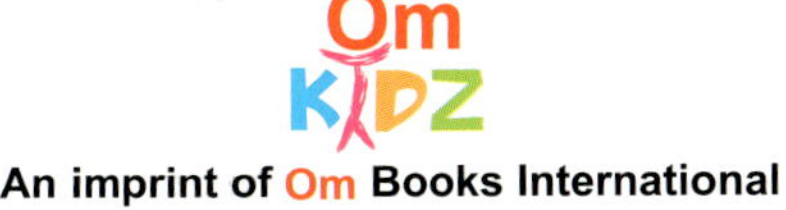

Published in 2017 by

An imprint of Om Books International

Corporate & Editorial Office
A 12, Sector 64, Noida 201 301
Uttar Pradesh, India
Phone: +91 120 477 4100
Email: editorial@ombooks.com
Website: www.ombooksinternational.com

Sales Office
107, Ansari Road, Darya Ganj, New Delhi 110 002, India
Phone: +91 11 4000 9000, 2326 3363, 2326 5303
Fax: +91 11 2327 8091
Email: sales@ombooks.com
Website: www.ombooks.com

ISBN: 978-93-86108-19-7

Printed in India

10 9 8 7 6 5 4 3 2 1

Time to SING

I'm all set to read

Paste your photograph here

My name is

Fil the fox loved to sing.

He sang by **the** river.

He sang under **the** tree.

He even sang **for Ben the bee**.

But Fil had a problem.

He **was not** very good at singing.

Ben did not mind. He **was** deaf.

He never could hear **Fil**.

One day, **Fil was** singing to **Ben**. Just then, Cora **the cow** walked by. **She** heard **him** sing.

“Oh my **God**, what **are you** doing?” **she** cried **out**.

"**Why**, I'm singing!" replied **Fil**.

"Don't **you** like my song?"

"This is **not** singing!" said Cora.

"This is what gives **you** an **ear** ache."

Fil felt very **sad**. Cora continued, "There, there! If **you** want to sing, **you** need to learn. **And** I know **the** perfect teacher **for you**!"

"**Who** would that be?" asked **Fil**.

“**Ori the owl**!” said Cora. “**She** will teach **you** a thing or **two** about singing.”

So **Fil** went to **Ori**. **She** lived in **the** hollow of a **big oak** tree.

“Hello, **Fil**!” said **Ori** when **she saw the fox**.

“What **can** I do **for you** today?”

“**Can you** teach me **how** to sing?” asked **Fil**.

“**Yes**, I **can**!” said **Ori**.

And she began to teach **him**.

“**One**, **two**, **let out** a toot.
Three, four, take **the** high note.”

Fil met Ori every **day**. **And** he learnt **and** he learnt until **his** singing **got** better.

Ori and Fil also became good friends.

"We should sing together!" said **Ori one day**.

"Really?" asked **Fil**. He **was** filled with excitement.

“**Yes**!” said **Ori**. “Let’s go to **the** forest square **and** sing **for** everyone!”

And so they went to **the** forest square. They **sat** on a **log and** began to sing.

"**Doe Ray** Me!

How happy **are** we!

So full of **joy**,

Under **the big** blue **sky**!"

All the animals gathered. **Ori and Fil** sang **one** song after another. When they finished, they took a **bow**. **All the** animals clapped with **joy**.

Ben the deaf **bee was** there **too**. He clapped **the** most **for Fil**!

"Well done, **Fil**. Well done, **Ori**. **You** should sing **new** songs **for** us every week!" said **the** animals.

Fil was very happy. He **had** finally learnt **how** to sing.

Circle the three-letter words from the tree below.

Change just one letter on each of these words and make new words!

Bow

______

Our

______

Had

______

Him

______

Log

______

Sad

______

Match these animals to their names.

Fil

Ori

Ben

Cora

Know your words

Sight Words

the him two joy
for God big all
but are can too
had you how new
was she and his
not out let doe
did why yes
one sad got
day who ray

Naming Words

Fil bee Ori log
fox cow owl bow
Ben ear oak sky

Doing Words

saw met sat